Big Bad Bill and the Swimming Pool

Bill was big.

Bill was bad.

"I am big bad Bill," said Bill.

Bill went to the pool.

"What bad thing can I do?" said Bill.

SWIM FOR IT!

Contents

Dee Reid

Story illustrated by
Andrew Painter

Heinemann

In this story

 Big Bad Bill

 The mum

 The little boy

Introduce these tricky words and help the reader when they come across them later!

Tricky words

- pool
- what
- thing
- splash
- really
- wave
- inflatable
- saved

Story starter

Big Bad Bill was big and bad. He loved to do bad things. One day, Big Bad Bill went to the swimming pool to find a bad thing to do.

"I see a bad thing I can do," said Bill.

"I can jump in the pool and make a big splash."

A little boy fell in the pool.

"Help! Help!" said the mum.
"My little boy fell in the pool."

Big Bad Bill made a big splash!
"I am really bad," said Bill.

The big splash made a big wave.

The big wave made the little boy go up, up, up.

The little boy went up on the inflatable.

"You saved my little boy,"
said the mum. "What a really
good thing to do."

The mum gave Big Bad Bill a *big* kiss.

"Yuk!" said Big Bad Bill.

12

Quiz

Text Detective

- Why did the mum give Big Bad Bill a kiss?
- Was Big Bad Bill bad?

Word Detective

- **Phonic Focus:** Blending three phonemes

  Page 3: Can you sound out 'bad'?
- Page 8: Find two words that are opposite in meaning.
- Page 10: Find a word meaning 'rescued'.

Super Speller

Read these words:

said   jump   fell

Now try to spell them!

HA! HA! HA!

Q What do you get when you cross a fish and an elephant?

A Swimming trunks!

13

Find out about

- The crazy challenge of swimming the English Channel

Tricky words

- people
- swimming
- challenges
- English Channel
- grease
- jellyfish
- charity
- fail

Introduce these tricky words and help the reader when they come across them later!

Text starter

Some people like to do crazy swimming challenges. One challenge is to swim the 21 miles across the English Channel. The sea is very cold and full of jellyfish.

Crazy Swimming!

Some people like to swim in a pool.

Some people like to swim in the sea.

Some people like to do crazy swimming challenges.

Swimming the English Channel is a crazy swimming challenge.

The sea is cold so the swimmers wear grease.

The grease keeps the swimmers warm.

The English Channel is full
of jellyfish.
The jellyfish sting the swimmers.

David Walliams is a TV star.
In 2006 David Walliams swam
the English Channel.

David Walliams swam the English Channel for charity. The charity got £1 million!

Lots of people try to swim
the English Channel.
Lots of people fail.

Would you do a crazy
swimming challenge?
Would you swim the
English Channel for £1 million?

Quiz

Text Detective

- Why is it difficult to swim the English Channel?
- Do you like swimming?

Word Detective

- **Phonic Focus:** Blending three phonemes
  Page 21: Can you sound out 'got'?
- Page 18: Find a word that rhymes with 'gold'.
- Page 19: Find a word made up of two words.

Super Speller

Read these words:

swim   cold   full

Now try to spell them!

HA! HA! HA!

Q What do swimmers eat off?

A A pool table.

24

Forward

Mary Kelly has lived and worked in Great Britain since 1968 and in that time has made an important contribution not only as an artist, but also as a teacher, writer, curator, and critic. All spheres of her activity are interrelated and project based, as such her art is consciously placed and directed within a context which seeks social change. It is an art which broke the bounds and unilateral direction of modernism to participate in wider debates concerning the nature of subjectivity, representation, sexuality, ideology and pleasure and which looked to psychoanalysis and its understanding of the human subject, to disentangle and to explore their mutual links. With subtlety and intelligence, the art exceeds the theory which is subsumed as part of the very substance and project of the work itself. A new space for the potential of art is opened out, using the very heterogeneity of society's discourses and the intricacy of their interplay to expose the multiplicity of structuring systems and cultural representations at work.

This publication coincides with the end of Mary Kelly's year as artist in residence at New Hall and Kettle's Yard, and with exhibitions of her work at both Kettle's Yard and Riverside Studios, London. The work presented is the first part of an ongoing piece with the overall title *Interim*. The work is composed of thirty panels, combining laminated photo positives, screenprints and painting on perspex. It was begun in 1983, completed in 1985, and first shown at The Fruitmarket Gallery, Edinburgh in the autumn of 1985. It will be seen for the first time in London at the Riverside Studios, whilst concurrently Kettle's Yard is exhibiting the preliminary art work (from which both the final work comes and the reproductions in this book were made) with a selection from the earlier work, *Post-Partum Document*, in order to emphasise the artist's working process.

Interim itself, in the words of the artist, looks at 'the moment of middle age' – that stage 'between' – and is based on over a hundred conversations with women which 'focus on the recurring themes of body, money, history and power'. Part I, *Corpus*, uses the discourses of fashion, popular medicine and romantic fiction to show how woman is defined primarily by her body in its procreative capacity and as a fetishised object, representations from which a woman in middle age is predominantly excluded. The thirty panels of paired image and text are divided into five sections entitled *Menacé, Appel, Supplication, Erotisme* and *Extase*, all terms employed by the French nineteenth century neuropathologist J. M. Charcot in his studies of female hysteria. They refer to the *attitudes passionelles* of the hysteric in the hallucinatory phase. In each section a complicated web of references leads to the progression, in both image and text, from a sense of neatness, order and superficial acceptability through suggested anxiety to disarray and confusion.

The extent and seductiveness of visual and textual references, even the scale (48″ x 36″) and presentation on reflective plexiglass of transparent images and the highly personal handwritten 'stories', all contribute to form a work of extraordinary tension and insight. Between order and disorder the tentative, disembodied questioning voice emerges with perceptive strength.

Many people must be thanked for their contributions towards the production of this publication and the exhibition of the work at The Fruitmarket Gallery, Kettle's Yard and Riverside Studios. We are grateful for Laura Mulvey's essay. We would also like to thank the artist for her attention and care at every stage throughout the production of the exhibitions and the publication; as artist in residence at New Hall and Kettle's Yard she has made an invaluable contribution both to the College and to the Gallery. Kettle's Yard itself would like to acknowledge the willingness and welcoming participation of the President and Fellows of New Hall in the Artist in Residence scheme; and also the generosity of the Arts Council in its funding. This residency represents the seventh organised by Kettle's Yard and importantly allows the artist a year in which to work without the burden of other commitments.

Finally but not least: The Fruitmarket Gallery acknowledges financial assistance from the Scottish Arts Council; Kettle's Yard from Eastern Arts, the Henry Moore Foundation, the Friends of Kettle's Yard and Cambridge City Council and Riverside Studios from the Arts Council of Great Britain, London Borough of Hammersmith and Fulham, the London Boroughs Grants Unit and the Stanley Thomas Johnson Foundation, Berne.

Hilary Gresty
Kettle's Yard

Mark Francis
The Fruitmarket Gallery

Milena Kalinovska
Riverside Studios

Impending time

CORPUS, the first section of Mary Kelly's large project INTERIM, conjures up something beyond the physical presence of the objects on display in the exhibition: emotions that cannot quite be pinned down into words, images that are on the verge of being discovered and ideas that are on the tip of a collective tongue. This sensation is central to the exhibition's subject and to its visual presentation. Both are allied closely to debate and experiment around women's relation to language and images that drew feminist aesthetics into 'alliance' with avant-garde aesthetics during the seventies. Mary Kelly's work as an artist and theorist, and my own work as a film-maker and theorist, are identified with this movement; and we both gained a cultural identity and frame-work from its existence. But our common political origins go back further, to the early days of the Women's Movement in 1970. It is for this reason that writing the introduction to this catalogue means more to me than the pleasure of discussing and celebrating the work of an artist I admire, and consider to have great political and poetic significance.

Paradoxically, our shared experience in the Women's Movement gives the exhibition a meaning for me that goes beyond the immediate constituency of feminist politics and aesthetics. The fact that we can now, from the perspective of 1986, look back to a common origin and involvement in a movement that has necessarily acquired a history, raises a plethora of speculations to do with time and then, questions about the political aspects of our concepts of time. These speculations are echoed in the actual content of the exhibition: the crisis of the female body at a certain age, and the crisis of representation caused by feminist resistance to images of the female body.

At first glance, CORPUS might seem to be about endings. Woman's beauty is like a *momento mori*, suggesting by its very perfection the inevitability of human decay. In a similar fashion, an avant-garde must be synonymous with innovation, validated by a gloss of novelty, and is thus stalked from its very inception by a threat of entropy and obsolescence. My own tendency, in the early to mid-eighties was to acquiesce in the death of the avant-garde. The conjuncture between radical politics and radical aesthetics that had been so important in the seventies seemed to have outlived its usefulness and should give way to the demands of time, trapped in the same destiny as a woman who loses her ability to desire as she accepts the world's surface estimation of her desirability.

At second glance, CORPUS specifically resists such a fatalistic closing off of an epoch into an ending. The exhibition is not about the woman *aged*, but about an INTERIM, an intermediate time during which the 'something' that might be pending can be transformed by changed understanding and perspectives so that it can be opened up to unexpected eventualities. Time is put 'on hold', as it were, and

stretched out for minute horizontal examination, not as a Canute-like resistance to the fact of passing time, but as a means of analysing the images and mythologies that predestine and constrain our experience of lived time. Similarly, Mary Kelly's aesthetic position seems to have avoided the avant-garde's proclivity to swing like a pendulum between the Scylla of purism on the margins and the Charybdis of recuperation at the centre. She also seems to have transcended the seventies paranoia about visual pleasure. Although there are numerous references to theory, and particularly the notoriously difficult psychoanalytic theory, there are other means of entry into understanding and enjoying the work. It is itself unashamedly beautiful and satisfying to the spectator. Without losing principle or intellectual rigour, poetry and visual experience are now immediate, giving hope for an avant-garde that can live beyond the founding moment of negative aesthetics. There is something opportune about this exhibition, as though Mary Kelly had, with a sixth sense, suggested that in considering the crisis of the woman's body as a construction in discourse, the seventies avant-garde needs to face its position in historical time and the critical, art-historical constructions that over-lay its presence as a movement.

Quite apart from the problems raised by an avant-garde's 'natural' life span, the transition from the seventies to the eighties has been particularly difficult. In retrospect the seventies have a self-contained identity. *Feminist* art and theory was born and became a self aware, articulate political and aesthetic project for the first time. There was an important coincidence between this transformative moment and a widespread reaction against the aesthetics of realism, echoing many aspects of feminist positions on representation and imagery. In the wider social and economic sphere, the seventies and the eighties are divided, with the effects of Thatcherism aggravating recession, unemployment, poverty, industrial crisis. It seems more appropriate in the exigencies of this situation, to turn away from the specialised issues of the seventies avant-garde to the real social and economic problems at hand. But there is something to be learnt, perhaps, from that other difficult and disastrous transition from the twenties to the thirties, when the politics of representation and concern with questions such as the representation of the unconscious fell from priority to irrelevance in the face of political and economic turmoil. Now it seems crucial not to abandon the feminist commitment to form as an area of struggle, since from a feminist perspective representation must be a political issue, while also reassessing the relation between art and politics at a time of historical change. And the feminist use of psychoanalytic theory has established that there is a reality of the psyche and collective fantasy that cannot be ignored. The aesthetics of heterogeneity that evolved during the seventies, allows different levels

Mary Kelly
Interim

The Fruitmarket Gallery, Edinburgh
30 November 1985 – 8 February 1986

Kettle's Yard Gallery, University of Cambridge
20 September – 24 October 1986

Riverside Studios, London
24 September – 19 October 1986

Published by The Fruitmarket Gallery, Kettle's Yard and Riverside Studios
Printed by Lecturis, Eindhoven

ISBN 0 907074 27 8
ISBN 0 947912 60 6

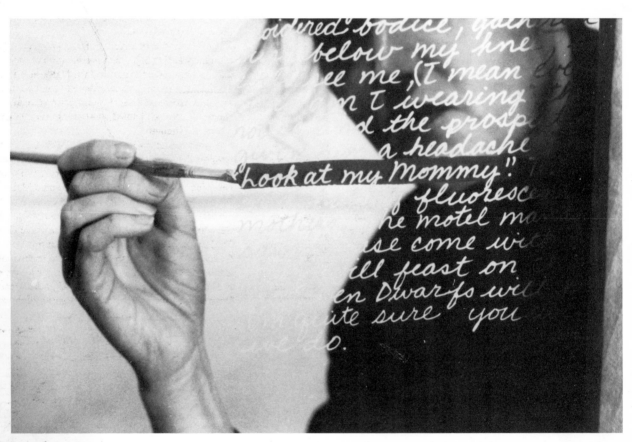

Mary Kelly working on Interim.

Installation, The Fruitmarket Gallery, Edinburgh, 1985.

of discourse to be juxtaposed, questioning a view of the world as a cohesive single strand that moves on a vertical axis through history. Now, in the eighties, heterogeneity must represent a vision of history itself as multi-layered, demanding differing points of perspective. The knight's move, detour through the unconscious, lack of synchronisation, are all strategies now associated with the post-modern that can also expand understanding of the relations between artistic practice and the social. For there is another danger, that fascination with the image as such, with the simulacrum's self-sufficiency might sever representation loose from its moorings to float on the surface of things in a passionate and relevant but isolated dialogue with itself. While the first part of INTERIM is undoubtedly about problems of representation and images, there is also a reference to a material and historical problem. The woman's body is not presented simply as an item of discourse, but lived in time and sexuality and emotion. There is a confidence in Mary Kelly's use of heterogeneity as a means to express poetic curiosity, and a rigorous uncertainty about the final answers to the issues she is raising.

There is also another problem of transition more specific to this artist. The theme of time in CORPUS can throw light back on to her previous work, POST PARTUM DOCUMENT, and the difficulties of moving on from there. Complicated and demanding, simultaneously monumental and as intricately woven as a tapestry, POST PARTUM DOCUMENT epitomises the theoretical asceticism of its time. It is about the space between birth and the Oepidus Complex that will end with her child's quasi understanding of his place in the historical dimension and his first inklings of the continuous, progressive nature of conscious visualisation of time. In contrast, the mother and child's dyadic relation is based on the experience of space in a continuous present tense.

> 'Infancy is a perpetual present. This could be linked with the small child's extraordinary memory – which is not a memory but a continuous actuality. So too, because of the Oedipus and Castration complexes, only humans have yesterdays. As far as we can tell neither animals nor pre-Oedipal human infants divide time into past, present, and future. Time for them would seem to be nearer to spatial relationships: here, there; come, gone; horizontal, punctuated duration rather than a vertical, temporal perspective.' (Juliet Mitchell: Introduction to
> *The Selected Melanie Klein)*

In addition to making the crucial distinction between temporal and spatial relations, this suggests more implicitly the way that our understanding of time is generally dependent on a visualisation, images in space, thus the sense of line and verticality as opposed to horizontal

punctuating points. In recent work on narrative structure, it has been usual to describe the cause/effect linearity of a story as a *horizontal* line of development. It is interesting to see how difficult but important the visualisation of process can be, how limited our conceptual vocabulary seems when it is needed. Within the aesthetic dimension, Maya Deren, in a famous symposium held in New York in 1963, tried to use the images of horizontal and vertical to distinguish between her conception of poetry and narrative:

> 'The distinction of poetry is its construction (what I mean by "a poetic structure"), and the poetic construct arises from the fact, if you will, that it is a "vertical" investigation of a situation, in that it probes the ramifications of the moment, and is concerned, in a sense, not with what is occurring, but what it feels like and what it means…' 'Now it may also include action, but its attack is what I would call a "vertical" attack, and this may be a little bit clearer if you contrast it to what I would call the "horizontal" attack of drama which is concerned with the development, let us say within a very small situation from feeling to feeling.'

It is not particularly important that Deren and Mitchell use their images of space/time in reverse. It is important that they are both evoking an imaginative space (poetry on the one hand and fantasy on the other) that exists alongside an image of vertical linearity, which only has space to acknowledge its own future destiny. (There is surely a place between these two quotations for Julia Kristeva's concept of the semiotic, in which she links the rhythms and patterns of poetry to the heterogeneity, the non-linearity, of the pre-Oedipal.) Juliet Mitchell later comments:

> The great theorists of the nineteenth century tradition – Darwin, Marx and Freud – explain the present by the past. The dominant sociological phenomenologies of the twentieth century in which Klein participated study lateral, horizontal, not vertical relationships.

It seems to me that feminist theory has mapped out another dimension to the 'lateral', bringing together the psycho-analytic, the political and the cultural. Perhaps above all, feminist theory has drawn attention to the area of contact between the unconscious and its manifestation on collective fantasy, roughly speaking, popular culture and representations. Freud, too, saw layers and levels to the human psyche, but the scars and traces that emerge symptomatically in language, images and symbolisations, as well as cultural phenomena, were to him, primarily, a means of interpreting and curing the present by means of the past. Feminism, on the other hand, as a political movement must endeavour to deconstruct, to question, to re-invent this terrain in which women's secondary status is sealed.

INTERIM focuses more specifically on this area than POST

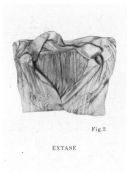
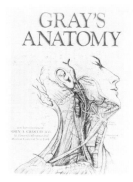

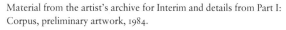

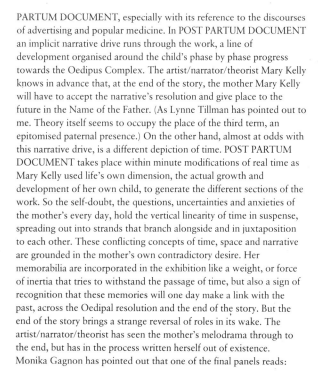

Material from the artist's archive for Interim and details from Part I:
Corpus, preliminary artwork, 1984.

PARTUM DOCUMENT, especially with its reference to the discourses
of advertising and popular medicine. In POST PARTUM DOCUMENT
an implicit narrative drive runs through the work, a line of
development organised around the child's phase by phase progress
towards the Oedipus Complex. The artist/narrator/theorist Mary Kelly
knows in advance that, at the end of the story, the mother Mary Kelly
will have to accept the narrative's resolution and give place to the
future in the Name of the Father. (As Lynne Tillman has pointed out to
me. Theory itself seems to occupy the place of the third term, an
epitomised paternal presence.) On the other hand, almost at odds with
this narrative drive, is a different depiction of time. POST PARTUM
DOCUMENT takes place within minute modifications of real time as
Mary Kelly used life's own dimension, the actual growth and
development of her own child, to generate the different sections of the
work. So the self-doubt, the questions, uncertainties and anxieties of
the mother's every day, hold the vertical linearity of time in suspense,
spreading out into strands that branch alongside and in juxtaposition
to each other. These conflicting concepts of time, space and narrative
are grounded in the mother's own contradictory desire. Her
memorabilia are incorporated in the exhibition like a weight, or force
of inertia that tries to withstand the passage of time, but also a sign of
recognition that these memories will one day make a link with the
past, across the Oedipal resolution and the end of the story. But the
end of the story brings a strange reversal of roles in its wake. The
artist/narrator/theorist has seen the mother's melodrama through to
the end, but has in the process written herself out of existence.
Monika Gagnon has pointed out that one of the final panels reads:

(What will I do?)
———————
S

poignantly foreseeing the gap left by the end of the work as well as the
loss of the dyad, and necessarily leading on to INTERIM.

Whereas POST PARTUM DOCUMENT had to accept narrative
closure, CORPUS makes an important contribution to opening out the
question of endings, both in the word and image panels. One of the
fascinating aspects of this work is its refusal to be pinned down or
categorised. Although the written texts are not arranged as
conventional stories, they contain many references to story-telling,
swerving from anecdote and recounting 'personal experiences' to the
fantastic world of fairy stories. The reader has to move from the
register of real life and its unobtainable desires to that of the
imagination where those desires can be 'lived out' in fantasy. In film,
feminists have, by and large, refused to follow extreme modernist
repudiation of narrative as such. Stories, myths and legends belong to

the structure of our collective fantasy and cannot be ignored. But
narrative also raises quite complex issues for feminism, particularly to
do with the active/passive, male/female distribution of functions
within a story and also the question of endings, of resolution to the
story line. Vladimir Propp has theorised the relation between character
and narrative function in folk tales. The hero's trials and tribulations
have a specific, stable point of departure and move through a series of
discrete points, a transformative process until he emerges triumphant
into a new stability at the end, a moment of heroic transcendence and
narrative resolution. Mary Kelly builds on the history of debate and
experiment that now exists as a body of work in this area, using it as a
spring board and reference point. Her central protagonist is drawn
more from the melodrama, the women's genre, which centres on a
heroine victim, and produces a particular kind of identification, based
on sympathy rather than idealisation. The overwhelming odds and
real, unresolvable problems that the victim protagonist faces can only
find a satisfactory 'ending' by unlikely, privileged good fortune, a
means of escape. This is the kind of narrative closure that Douglas Sirk
cites as the 'deus ex machina' or 'tying the story together neatly with
pink ribbons'. The artifice is clear to the spectator/reader. Mary Kelly
draws unerringly on this tradition when she ends her series of written
texts in Disneyland and 'they lived happily ever after'. She brings
together the Proppian structure and its recognition of the importance
of endings with the melodrama's ironic undermining of them. Both the
fairy story and the melodrama depend on transition from a state of
misfortune to happiness. The misfortune is usually grounded in
recognisable conditions of oppression, the world's injustice to those
without power. The state of happiness is manifestly really only to be
achieved through collective imagination. *Corpus* is both documentary
and fantasy. Alongside the references to fairy tales, the discourses of
advertising, popular medicine and romantic fiction is the presence of
the tape-recorder. The stories vividly reflect women's real dilemmas
and the hand-written texts are reminiscent of a diary, but they are also
images, textures, traces of the body in an emblematic sense.

At another level this combination of the real with fantasy refers to
the analytic process itself, with its illusive double register both in an
individual's experience of real events and the invisible processes of the
unconscious. References to psychoanalysis as a discourse and a history
run through the whole work. The images, arranged in five sets of
three, are named after the poses that Charcot identified as expressing
the symptoms of sexual desperation in his hysterical female patients,
and sets up two different historical traditions. First there is the history
of psychoanalysis and its founding conversion from the study of the
physical symptom (Charcot) to the study of word and language
(Freud). There is also the history of psychoanalysis within feminism,

Attitudes Passionelles-Extase, plate from *Iconographie de la Salpêtrière*, J.M. Charcot, 3 volumes, Paris 1877-80.

and its origins, particularly the early, intuitive fascination with hysteria as specific to women and their sexual oppression under patriarchy. (Freud's case history 'Dora' is a pivot point for both these histories and Mary Kelly refers to the further problem of Dora's relation to her mother in the final set of texts.) Both psychoanalysis and feminism desire to be transformative. In terms of narrative theory they belong to the middle section of a story where change, adventures and traumas are acknowledged, within a time structure but one that questions the inevitability of closure and resolution, a challenged aspiration towards a stable point at the end of a 'correct line' of development.

The triptych structure in CORPUS has a further aesthetic dimension. The first two images are closely linked together in a binary structure. The first encapsulates masquerade, the glossy finish of Hitchcock's blonde heroines, a pervasive presence in advertising which condenses woman's relation to commodity circulation and her own tendency to commodification. The second image tears off the mask to reveal a hidden disorder, the body and its actual uncontrolable symptoms. In the garments, their arrangement and their relation to women's speech/writing and still unspeakable desire, CORPUS achieves a very fine balance between the iconoclastic repression of the body during the seventies and a present recognition that its political and aesthetic place within feminism must be acknowledged and expressed. But it is wrong to over-emphasise the dependent relations of the first two images. The presence of the third breaks into the neat duality that constructs our mythologies into polarisations such as public/private, inside/outside, voyeurism, exhibitionism, mother/whore, masculinity/femininity and so on. The third image, with its explicit sexual reference to a discourse of perversion, opens up the question, beyond the balance between surface attraction, desirability, and inner physical and emotional feeling to the problem of female sexual desire. Mary Kelly implies that desire cannot be expressed without an image that can represent it. This third panel then, speaks to the future, to the common need to redefine *women's* relation to their image, beyond the question of male appropriation of their image for masculine pleasure, to discover a feminine desire and understand female sexuality. The question, the gap, therefore, is addressed to 'us'.

Laura Mulvey

MARY KELLY

Born in Minnesota, 1941
Pius XII Institute, Florence, Italy, MA, 1963-65
St Martin's School of Art, London, 1968-70

Awards
Arts Council Award, 1977
Lina Garnade Memorial Foundation Award, 1978
Greater London Arts Association Visual Arts Award, 1980

Appointments
Greater London Arts Association Visual Arts Panel, 1977-79
Editorial Board, *Screen Magazine,* 1979-81
Selector, *New Contemporaries,* Institute of Contemporary Arts,
London, 1982
Advisory Board, *m/f* 1982-86
Curator, *Beyond the Purloined Image,* Riverside Studios, London, 1983
Artist in Residence, New Hall and Kettle's Yard, Cambridge University,
1985-86

Public Collections
Kunsthaus Zürich
Arts Council of Great Britain
Australian National Gallery, Canberra
Tate Gallery, London
New Hall, Cambridge University

Publications by the Artist
Notes on reading the Post-Partum Document, *Control,* 10, 1977
'Women's Practice in Art', *Audio Arts,* vol. 3, no. 3, 1977
'The State of British Art', *Studio International,* 2, 1978
'On Femininity', *Control,* 11, 1979
'Sexual Politics', *Art and Politics,* Winchester School of Art Press, 1980
'Re-viewing Modernist Criticism', *Screen,* 22/3, 1981
'Feminist Art: Assessing the 70's and raising issues for the 80's', *Studio
International,* 195, 991/12, 1981
'Documentation VI', *m/f,* 5 & 6, 1981
'Post-Partum Document', *Sense and Sensibility,* Midland Group,
Nottingham, 1982
'Beyond the Purloined Image', *Block,* 9, 1983
Post-Partum Document, Routledge & Kegan, Paul, London, 1983
'Jenseites des entwendeten Bildes', *Archithese,* 5, 1983
'Desiring Images/Imaging Desire', *Wedge,* 6, 1984
'Post-Scriptum', The *Critical Eye/I,* Yale Center for British Art,
New Haven, 1984
'Re-viewing Modernist Criticism', (reprint), *Art after Modernism,* New
Museum of Contemporary Art, New York; D.R. Godine, Boston, 1984
'Interim', (five part series) *The Guardian* June 2, 9, 16, 23 & 30, 1986
'Mary Kelly in Conversation with Laura Mulvey', *Afterimage,* 1986

ONE-PERSON EXHIBITIONS (and selected reviews)

1976
Institute of Contemporary Arts New Gallery, London, *Post-Partum
Document.*
        Laura Mulvey, *Spare Rib,* 53, 1976,
        Richard Cork, *Evening Standard,* October 14, 1976
        Jane Kelly, *Studio International,* 193, no. 985, 1/1977

1977
Museum of Modern Art, Oxford, *Post-Partum Document,*
        Catalogue: *Footnotes and Bibliography: Post-Partum
        Document* by the artist
        Sarah Kent, *Time Out, December* 30, 1977
        Mark Nash, *Artscribe,* 10, 1978
1979
University Gallery, Leeds, *Post-Partum Document*
New 57 Gallery, Edinburgh, *Post-Partum Document*
1981
Anna Leonowens Gallery, Halifax, *Post-Partum Document*
        Jo-Anna Isaak, *Vanguard,* 11, April, 1982
1982
George Paton Gallery, Melbourne, *Post-Partum Document*
        Freda Freiburg, *Lip,* 7, 1983
University Art Museum, Brisbane, *Post-Partum Document*
1985
The Fruitmarket Gallery, Edinburgh, *Interim*
        Alice Bain, *The List,* December, 1985
        Edward Gage, *The Scotsman,* December, 1985
1986
A Space, Toronto, *Interim*
        Carole Corbeil, *Toronto Globe and Mail,* March 20, 1986
        Diedre Hanna, *Now,* no. 28, March, 1986
        Monika Gagnon, C, Summer, 1986
Kettle's Yard Gallery University of Cambridge, *Selected Works*
        Catalogue with essay by Laura Mulvey
Riverside Studios, London, *Interim*

GROUP EXHIBITIONS (and catalogue essays)

1975
Northern Arts Gallery, Newcastle, *Sexuality and Socialisation*
South London Art Gallery, London, *Women & Work: A Document on
the Division of Labor in Industry*
1977
Art Net, London, *Radical Attitudes to the Gallery*
        Published in Studio International, 195, no. 900, 1980
1978
Whitechapel Art Gallery, London, *Art for Society* traveled to Ulster
Museum, Belfast
Hayward Gallery, London, *Hayward Annual '78*
        Catalogue by Lucy Lippard and Sarah Kent
1979
ARC, Musée d'Art Moderne de la Ville de Paris, Paris, *Un Certain
Art Anglais*
        Catalogue essay by Mark Nash
Hetzler, Müller & Schurr, Stuttgart, *Europa '79*
        Kunstforum (Mainz), no. 36, 1979 special review issue
Haags Gemeentemuseum, The Hague, *Feministische Kunst
Internationaal;* traveled to de Oosterpoort, Groningen, Noordbrabants
Museum, Den Bosch, de Vleeshal, Middelburg, de Vest, Alkmaar,
De Beyerd, Breda, and Nijmeegs Museum, Nijmegen
        Catalogue essays by Din Pieters and Rosa Lindenburg
Artemesia Gallery, Chicago, *Both Sides Now*
Artists Space, New York, *British Art*
Kettle's Yard, Cambridge, *Verbiage*
Dartington College of Art, Totnes, *Art, Politics & Ideology*

1980
Institute of Contemporary Arts, London, *Issue: Social Strategies by Woman Artists*
        Catalogue essay by Lucy Lippard
1981
Bonner Kunstverein and Gallery Magers, Bonn, *Typisch Frau*; traveled to Städtische Galerie
Biuro Wystaw Catalogue Artystycznuch, Cracow, *9th Cracow Meetings*
Woodlands Art Gallery, London, *Greater London Arts Association Touring Exhibition*
1982
Art Gallery of New South Wales, Sydney, *Vision in Disbelief: 4th Biennale of Sydney*
Midland Group Gallery, Nottingham, *Sense and Sensibility*
        Catalogue essay by Griselda Pollock
1983
Protetch McNeil, New York, *The Revolutionary Power of Women's Laughter;* traveled to Art Culture Resource Center, Toronto and Washington College Art Gallery, Maryland
        Essay statement by Jo Anna Isaak
1984
Yale Center for British Art, New Haven, *The Critical Eye/I*
        Catalogue by John T. Paoletti
City of Birmingham Museum and Art Gallery and Ikon Gallery, *The British Art Show;* traveled to Royal Scottish Academy, Edinburgh, Mappin Art Gallery, Sheffield and the Southampton Art Gallery
        Catalogue essay by Jon Thompson
The New Museum of Contemporary Art, New York, *Difference: On Representation and Sexuality;* traveled to the Renaissance Society University of Chicago, Illinois, Massachusetts Institute of Technology Boston and the Institute of Contemporary Arts, London
        Catalogue essays by Craig Owens and Lisa Tickner
1986
Public Access Project, Toronto, *Some Uncertain Signs*
Collins Gallery University of Strathclyde, *Identity/Desire: Representing the Body,* traveled to Crawford Centre for the Arts, St. Andrews and McLaurin Art Gallery, Ayr

GENERAL BIBLIOGRAPHY

1978
Terence Maloon, 'Interview with Mary Kelly', *Artscribe,* 13
Jane Kelly, 'Mary Kelly', *Studio International,* 3 1979
Jasia Reichardt, 'The Use of Sources', *Skira Annual* 5, 1979

1980
Richard Cork, 'Collaboration without Compromise', *Studio International,* 990
Judith Barry, Sandy Flitterman, 'The Politics of Art Making', *Screen,* 21, 2
Alexis Hunter, 'Feminist Perceptions', *Artscribe,* 25

1981
Elizabeth Cowie, 'Introduction to the Post-Partum Document', *m/f,* 5 & 6
Margaret Iverson, 'The Bride Stripped Bary by Her Own Desire', *Discourse,* 4, UCLA Berkeley
Rozsika Parker, Griselda Pollock, *Old Mistresses: Women , Art and Ideology,* Routledge and Kegan Paul, London
Helen Grace, 'From the Margins: A Feminist Essay on Women Artists', *Lip,* 2

1982
Paul Smith, 'No Essential Femininity' (Paul Smith in conversation with Mary Kelly), *Parachute,* 26
Paul Smith, 'Mother as the Site of Her Proceedings', *Parachute,* 26
Paul Taylor, 'The 4th Biennale of Sydney', *Artforum,* XXI, October

1983
Lip Collective, 'Dialogue', *Lip,* 7
Kate Linker, 'Representation and Sexuality', *Parachute,* 32
Margaret Iverson, 'Post-Partum Document und die Lageder post-moderne', *Archithese,* 5
Jean Fisher, 'Beyond the Purloined Image', *Art Forum,* December
Jane Weinstock, 'A Laugh, A Lass and A Lad', *Art in America,* Summer

1984
Craig Owens, 'The Discourse of the Others: Feminists and Post-Modernism', *The Anti-Aesthetic,* Bay Press, Washington
Kate Linker, 'Eluding Definition', *Art Forum,* December
Sheena Gourlay, 'The Discourse of the Mother', *Fuse,* summer
Caroline Osbourne, 'The Post-Partum Document', *Feminist Review,* winter
Deborah Bershad, 'The Post-Partum Document', *Critical Texts,* Columbia University
Lucy Lippard, *Get the Message,* E.P. Dutton, New York

1985
John Paoletti, 'Mary Kelly's Interim', *Arts,* October
Jane Weinstock, 'A Post-Partum Document', *Camera Obscura,* 13, 14
Paul Smith, 'No Essential Femininity' (reprint), *Camera Obscura,* 13, 14
Griselda Pollock, 'History and Position of the Contemporary Woman Artist', *Aspects,* 28
Sarah Kent and Jacqueline Morreau, *Images of Men,* Readers and Writers, London
Mark Lewis, 'Concerning the Question of the Post-Cultural', *C,* winter
Jo Anna Isaak, 'Women: The Ruin of Representation', *Afterimage,* April

1986
Andrea Fraser, 'On the Post-Partum Document', *Afterimage,* March
Margaret Iverson, 'Difference on Representation and Sexuality', *m/f,* 11 & 12
Paul Smith, 'Difference in America', *Art in America,* April

MENACÉ

The room is crowded yet subdued, almost silent. No music, no dancing. Everyone is talking quietly in couples or small groups. Many are old friends, some I haven't seen for several years. They look different, not just greyer or fatter or more degenerate or less fashionable, just not the same. We are celebrating Lynn's fortieth birthday. "You look great," she says, kissing me on both cheeks, "haven't changed at all," then Anna mocks us but affectionately, "well preserved." She smiles. We laugh. I am content. Embalmed by the warmth, the comfort of their compliments, immutable, at least until Ros whispers, "How old are you anyway?" and I remember I am nearly forty-three. I hesitate and Sarah fills the gap with, "See, she can't even say it!" A possible reprieve, Elizabeth, comes over and asks me what I'm working on. I tell her it's another long project and hope she won't pursue it. "On what," she insists. I fumble, knowing it will sound dreadful no matter how I say it, "middle-age, well, that is, I suppose I mean women like us." "I don't feel middle-aged," she snaps, seems offended. I try to explain that it's not so literal, more about the way we represent it to ourselves, almost before the fact. She says she has a phobia about it, tries to change the subject. Sarah interrupts to tell me the leather jacket is lovely but she distinctly remembers that I said I'd never wear one. I confess I finally gave in for professional reasons, that there's so much to think about now besides what to wear, that the older you are the harder it seems to be to get it right and that the uniform makes it a little easier. I look at Maya for confirmation but she disagrees, says there's a certain freedom attached to getting older, not caring so much, being able to get up in the morning and get dressed like a man, confidently, without wasting time primping. I notice she is dressed simply, hair hanging loosely on her shoulders, wearing very little make-up, nearly sixty and absolutely gorgeous. I say I'm not so sure most men are that secure but maybe her confidence comes from knowing she has always been a very attractive woman. She looks surprised. "No one is that confident," she protests, "I must admit I've never missed an opportunity to glance in a mirror as I passed it, or in a shop window, or any reflective surface for that matter, hoping to catch a glimpse of myself as others see me." Lynn is lighting the candles, "Watch me," she says, "I'm going to blow them out now." And she does, all forty, without a flicker.

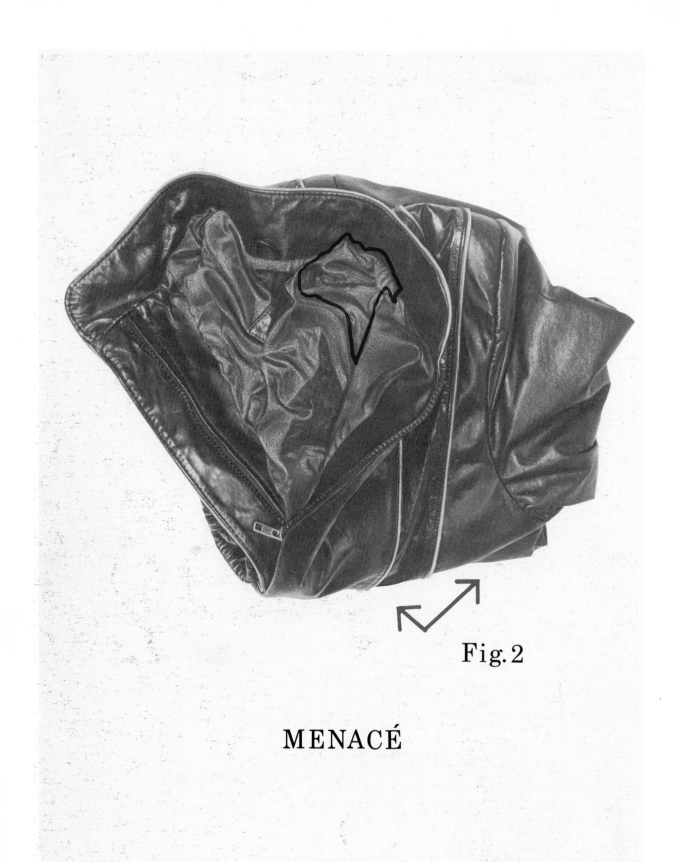

Fig. 2

MENACÉ

The clinic is nearly empty. I am waiting, heart beating, the bell rings, I go in. "Take off your clothes and put this on," he says, "I'll be back in a few minutes." I want to explain first but it's too late, he's gone. I rehearse it. Don't want another child, no can't afford another child, have professional commitments. No, that won't impress him. My first child is almost nine, too old to have another one? He's back, "How old are you? Do you have any children? When was your last period?" He won't listen, just the facts. Preoccupied with looking, only the evidence. "This won't take long," he says. "Relax." Can't relax, can't talk, can't see. Blind spot. Whose? I ask myself on his behalf. Yours, theirs? No one will talk about it. About what? Pregnancy? No. Menstruation? No, not exactly. Something less specific, secret places, secretions, odd swellings, strange smells, odors, lack of order, disorder, being older? I remember Clara saying that the reason older women often give for having an abortion is not wanting the other children to know. To know what? That she laughs too loudly, eats too much, has sex, desires? It's not becoming to be coming, not at her age anyway. It would be so obvious, obvious in my case that I'm procrastinating, not serious about my work. "Too soon to tell," he doesn't smile, "We'll have to wait. The lab will send results next week. Ring then." Can't wait. I say I have an important lecture to give, must leave the country by the end of the week, but he isn't listening. Now he isn't even looking. I know he's thinking that's irrelevant, why is this woman so hysterical. I feel like crying. I always feel like crying. This is ridiculous. He hands me the plastic bottle, the white label, the facts, the evidence, "You can get dressed now."

Menacé

The music is loud, too loud to talk. Sound swells and breaks, rolling over me, through me, funky, dissonant, feels good. I want to dance, smile at Ruth soliciting a partner. We push our way into the center of the room and start to move in what I think is perfect unison, except that from a certain position I can see myself in the cloakroom mirror. The image grates. I keep manœuvering back to it for a replay, seems so out of synch with how I feel. The clothes perhaps, not tough enough, too sixties. No, the hair, too severe, should fly across my face when I turn. No, it's more insidious than that, the expression is wrong, too animated, childish even, absurd at my age. Keep the mouth closed and look cynical to compensate for the double chin. Beware of raising your arms and unleashing untidy ripples of loose flesh that linger thereon. No, the hips, definitely the hips, hardly perceptible but not quite the same, something to do with the feeling of space around the waist. Ruth has gone for a drink and someone is offering me a joint. I feel silly. Everyone I know went back to alcohol years ago. Still, everyone I know is thousands of miles away and everyone here is so Goddamn young. Mostly students. I feel like a chaperone. Aren't there any other lecturers for Chrissake. I spot a post-graduate fellow, greying at the temples, looks promising. I corner him. He says he's a feminist so I proceed to ramble on about the beginnings of the women's movement saying, "You remember the first meeting at Oxford, don't you?" "No," he says, "I was fourteen in 1968." I am stunned, can't speak, feel deceived. How can he know so much? Why does he look like that? Thirty-five at the very least, but twenty-seven? It's hopeless. I'm reduced to a voyeur. Besides, he's with someone who looks like less than twenty-one. I hate them. He senses it, hands me another drink. For a moment, I imagine that he is Prince Gold Hand bringing the Old Crone a glass of the Water-that-makes-Young from the Fourth Well and I croak, "Have you got it, have you got it?" "Yes," he replies and I seize it in my wizened hands, pour it over me and immediately turn into a beautiful maiden. Then, I ask him what he would like as an offering of thanks, but he says he can't think of anything because the Princess is all he desires and she is already standing with her hand in his. At this point, of course, I want to turn them both into frogs and vanish from their sight forever. But instead, I just excuse myself and go to look for Ruth.

15

APPEL

The waiter is taking our coats. Jan admires my bag and asks me where I got it. "Can't remember." I explain it's not that I don't care, just that I don't have time to shop that systematically. "It may sound trivial," she says, surveying the menu, "but the way people look is important." "It does seem trivial," I tell her, diverting my eyes from the entrées. "It's a form of identification...," she orders a salad. Jean does the same, then interprets, "..based on rather conventional notions like pretty or cute, attractive or striking...," "Absurdly simple," I complain, but can't resist. "Examples?" Jan obliges with Teena's cute, Kay striking, Sophie attractive but not striking and Jean is pretty. Jean smiles. The salads arrive. They look striking, but not terribly attractive. "What about Tricia?" I challenge her. "Difficult," she admits, "but probably just sixties sexpot." I am shocked, but laugh anyway, "And Marty?" "Sixties too," she pauses, "yet unique, a self-styled slob." Now I am worried, stop laughing, stab a lettuce leaf and tell her that I wouldn't want to be considered pretty, it sounds too insipid. "Well, you're not," she says, must think I meant it. I feel helpless. They're so much younger, don't understand. I need evidence. Yes, the college photo. No, that was more than fifteen years ago. What would it prove, only that I am quite humorless about the whole thing and refuse to grow old gracefully. Must rise above it. Be clever, useful, interesting. "Accept the fact that you no longer charm someone by simply looking good." She tries to be consoling now, "You're more like me," she says, "attractive, even striking sometimes." Improbable comparison, she knows it—sleek, shining Aphrodite of the eighties sitting there sipping her Perrier, confident that she is never less than striking. The waiter returns. She refuses dessert, coffee too. He looks at me, still hungry but I say, "No thanks." The bill, my bag, I'm pleased she likes it, proves at least I have good taste. Still hungry though, want something else. The past? Yes please, a small, sweet slice will do.

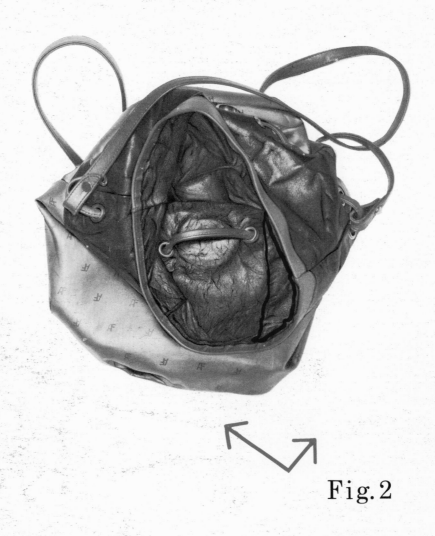

Fig.2

APPEL

It's late and I'm looking up an emergency treatment for cystitis in a self-help manual called "Woman's Body". The index directs me to L 23. En route I catch a glimpse of a hideous diagram, keep going, then turn back, M 4: The Process of Aging. What do I find so compelling about this graphic destruction of the female figure from age 0 to 80. I resist. She looks much too old for 50, obviously based on the down-to-earth-had-a-hard-life-and-glad-its-over type. I will never look like that, or will I? Brutal, statistical fact, there it is. I am reducible to example d) middle age: muscle strength and mental capabilities past their prime. So my son had a point asking me if I would still be able to play with him when I was 40. Though it could be worse, e) fertility ceases, and then f) old age: spine drops, hearing impaired, character changes and brain disorders possible. God, why go on. It's already started. Is it irreversible? Anne told me she could remember the exact day, hour even, when she became an older woman. One morning she woke up, looked down at her breasts and realized they had lost their independence. She was laying on her side, she emphasized the importance of her vantage point since it was in that very position she had previously observed two perfectly autonomous hemispheres defying the laws of gravity. That day, they sloped, no, she said slithered to the right as they surrendered to some imperious genetic signal saying "take a break." I asked how old she was and had to laugh when she said 25. But now, reading in reverse I notice c) continuous loss of nerve cells from the age of 25, then b) peak of physical energy over at 12. Finally their optimistic introduction, "The aging process begins suprisingly early and efforts to slow it down are simply guesswork". Organic, inevitable, yet we are obsessed with avoiding it. Anne is right, women are not at one with nature, they are at war with it. The victor becomes a legend like so many aging film stars, forever "Fabulous and Forty-two"; meanwhile, the vanquished who refuse to dye their hair or just don't give a damn become old bags, or possibly old ladies if they smile.

X _mk_

Appel

She glances at the menu, then at the door, intent but not impatient. "Sorry I'm late," I begin to make excuses, "Never mind, you waited last time," she embraces me, "it's good to see you." Her presence calms me as it always has, for nearly fifteen years. I ask her if that's possible. She says it must be since we met in 1968. Then we sail across the crowded harbour and cast anchor at our favorite table, our island by the window where we reminisce; then plan. Do the translation, exchange the manuscripts, write the article, promote the project, her project my project, our intervention. But first, we order two hors' oeuvres and savour compliments about our clothes, our hair, then launch complaints about our lovers, them, the men, uncomprehending others on the mainland, distant, unpredictable, paling to insignificance against our monument – unfailing friendship. After that, as usual we share one dessert, have many cups of coffee and give good advice. "I'll tell you something if you promise not to say a word to anyone," she looks elated. "So you've finally found the right one?" "Don't be cynical, I can't help thinking that there must be something better, something more." "And is there?" "Yes, and no, but now I don't know what to do." "Because he's married?" "Mmm." I tell her to forget it, stop procrastinating, finish the book. "The problem is, you have a Don Juan Complex." "Don Juanita," she corrects me and we laugh. Same familiar conversation, same delicious laughter. She goes on, "Don't you ever wonder what you're missing?" "Yes, but work is all that matters at the moment." "Well, a change might help." "The only change I need is time to do it." "Then, stop teaching." Seems so easy, so convincing when she says it. "And the money?" "Let him make it for a while." Absurd idea, and still, I want to hear it. They are closing, asking us to leave. The light is almost gone. Somehow the island now looks greener, fresher, but the seagulls sound more mournful. I protest, "We've just begun." The manuscript, the article, the buried treasure. "Next time," we both agree. I take her arm and then look back, everything two girls could long for – a boat, a cave, a castle and someone else to do the cooking. "Could there ever be another place as wonderful as this?" "Of course not," she replies.

SUPPLICATION

Phone rings, goes on her way. Glad she's coming, though I met her only once before at the museum. Winter, ground covered in ice, everything about to crack, fragile, intense — her performance, my ordeal with the director, our conversation over breakfast. Wonder if she still remembers, if she's changed. Lovely dancer's body in baggy pants, huge leather jacket, lace-up boots, all carefully battered like her face, small features more defined with some success, emblazoned. Live alone, a loft downtown of course, no nonsense baby, if you want to be an artist you must pay. I am in debt, no doubt about it, overdressed and uncommitted, wishing I could seek asylum in her duffle bag. Stunned by the 'rightness' of that image first, then intrigued by every detail, but especially by the boots. They had a presence much like hers, older but not dated and attractive without trying too hard. They haunted me. I had to have them, kept on looking for months after, finally found some that were similar, not soulfully worn out but stylishly distressed at least. In these I could do anything, wore them all the time, have them on now in fact. Will she be wearing hers? The door. I let her in, look down — the boots are different, lighter, higher heels and polished. Then look up — astonishing, a dress, small flowers, forties, second-hand, cut on the bias, screaming: what the hell, feels good to be a woman sometimes, give me credit I'll pay later. And the jacket, padded shoulders, Persian lamb, not black but very much like mine, the one that I was wearing when we met. She senses this and says that's why she bought it, tried to look smart, stylish even, just to please me. Can't help smiling, "See these boots," I ask, "have I succeeded?" "Well, almost," she laughs.

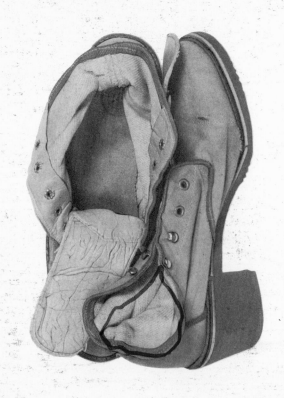

Fig.2

SUPPLICATION

Summer arrives. Suddenly it's hot and we need bathing suits, go shopping, try on several hundred of them so it seems but nothing fits. They're either too small on top and too big on the bottom, or too big on top and too small on the bottom, or too small altogether, especially if we like them. "It was never this difficult when we were younger," I complain, "everything just seemed to look good, I don't understand it, nothing is right." We are looking in the mirror. I blame the angle of reflection, lighting, anything, but can't accept that that is me. Elena says she sees her mother and is horrified by the resemblance, "It was such a shock to see her growing older, now I can't help thinking, do I look like that already?" "No, of course not," I assure her. But the children interrupt us, they are restless, anxious to go swimming. We are wasting time, and sun, it will be gone if we don't hurry. She makes up her mind to wear an old suit and forget it. I don't have one, so decide to use my underwear, why not, it's black and much more flattering besides. The beach is crowded, but the sun feels warm and healing. In the future we'll look better, with a little effort. At the moment we are happy. There are other things that give us pleasure. Yes, the children, they are lovely. See how much they are enjoying this? We smile. Then, "Mum", a small voice shouts, "your legs are fat." Elena laughs and I begin to lecture, "Look," I say, "if you compared my fat legs with all the fat legs over forty, you'd discover..." but he's gone before I finish so I carry on complaining to Elena, asking her what can be done to fight the dreaded flabby thigh. She points in the direction of her beach bag where I see a Sunday paper, take it out and note the Supplement devoted to the preservation of the perfect pair of legs : first, you should jog for at least fifteen minutes everyday; follow this with one hour's arduous exercise; then thirty minutes of massage, pedicure recommended, waxing optional but resting absolutely necessary, legs raised, ankles on a cushion for not less than twenty minutes, preferably at midday. "You see." Elena says, "it's very simple, all you have to do is dedicate your whole life to it."

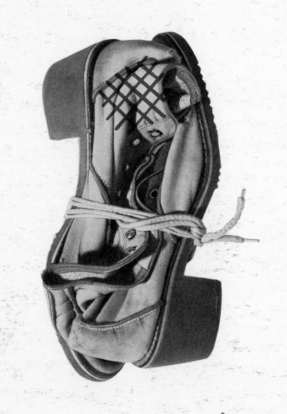

Supplication

No time. Well, yes, a drink. It could be useful; his work, my work, other shows perhaps? No deal. I know it now that we are sitting here across the table from each other smiling so excessively my mouth begins to ache. There is really no relationship, no reason to pursue this. But he smiles sweetly, eyes are blue, they sparkle when he says, "You're such a lovely person." I become a landscape, yes of course, dark continent to be discovered, faithful wife and loving mother, maybe even artist's muse. I'm not annoyed somehow, but flattered, must be getting older. A true artist so he tells me, doesn't live in New York City, doesn't seek success, it finds him. Not to say he is religious just believes, religiously, in art. Great art is not a product of the mind, but of the hand and heart. He asks still smiling, "Would you like another drink?" And I say, "yes". No reason. But I want to. I feel good, soft, edible and slightly heart-shaped. Wonder if he's wearing his best jacket just for me. No time. No reason to pursue this, work to do, it's nearly midnight. "Tell me," he leans over, "what you're thinking," meaning please stop thinking dammit, lovely person. Thinking is a dangerous practice. Eyes still sparkling he suggests, "Lets go to my place, have a coffee where it's quiet, we can talk..." "I can't." "Why not." "I didn't plan on it." He says he did, for several months. I'm taken by surprise but now inflexible; absurd at my age. I feel flushed and rather foolish, want to stay but say I'm sorry. Call a taxi, comes ten silent minutes later; body painted gold, interior lined with velvet. Odd. I ask the driver who is dressed in purple livery and looks vaguely like a lizard, if there's some mistake. I didn't want a limousine and can't afford it. He assures me it's alright, he's just eccentric. I get in, lean back, spread out my satin skirt across the seat, slip off my silver pumps and think. Should have stayed, no reason not to. It's too late. The radio announces twelve o'clock, the car breaks down, the lizard scurries off and I walk home in rags and wooden shoes.

ÉROTISME

A winter evening. We're sitting by the fire and Vance is telling us a story. Once there was a woman whom he found attractive, but as it happened, he'd never seen her wearing make-up. This puzzled him, so he discussed it with a friend who suggested that perhaps she didn't need it. "Until then," he muses, "it never occurred to me to wonder whether a woman needed it or not." We shake our heads and start to speak at once, "I disagree," we chant. "With what?" he shrugs. "With need," he says, "it isn't functional." "Why not?" he asks. "Because the flaw," she tells him, "isn't real, it's imagined, so it can't be covered up." He looks confused. She turns to me. I smile at him, "Well, no one can convince a woman that her imperfection isn't there. Her standard of beauty, I suppose, is···" "Absolute," he interrupts. "Meaning what?" he is sincere. "Meaning so internalized that it seems arbitrary," she explains. "Make-up or not," I add, "it's all the same, nothing to do with function or with fashion, even less to do with pleasing men. The only clue would be her mother." "When I was young," he stages it, "I really did like lipstick, used to spend hours thinking about how I could get it to stay on. Then I went through my puritan phase. Now I'm too old to care, so I've decided to please myself." "For me," Vance thinks out loud, "the way I look is just a means of getting what I want···" he pauses, grins, "the usual, sex and money." We laugh. I sermonize, "For us, in fact it often costs alot in terms of our profession and our personal lives," then look at him. "The only satisfaction that we get," she sighs, "is knowing that for such persistent efforts there are moments when it comes off well." "I see," he stares into the fire. It crackles and we hear applause.

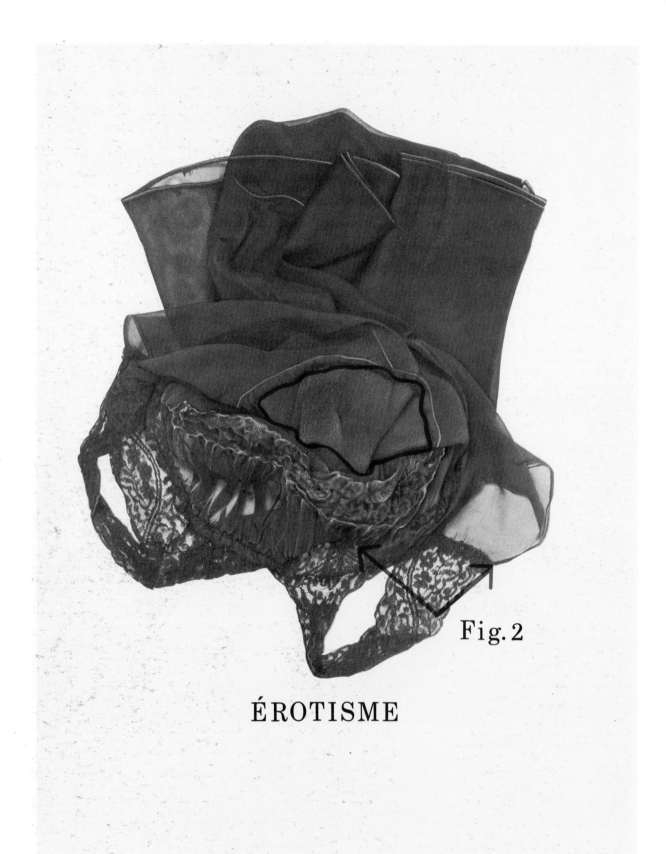

Fig. 2

ÉROTISME

Outside it's cold, raining again. Inside it's nearly eighty-five, palm trees, screeching parrots and stripped pine everywhere. "The Sanctuary" Elena finally convinced me, shouldn't let myself go, might even enjoy it. Perhaps. The heat is soothing, but the back-to-natureness is slightly nauseating. I have second thoughts. Too late, already issued with a locker key and look of condescension that makes me want to say I'm sorry, my first time. For what, I wonder, glancing at a pamphlet — two naked blondes, shoulders back, tits pressed together, bottoms protruding in perfect symmetry against a black background, gleaming presumably from aromotherapy oils, the caption, "Ladies Only Health Club." That has nothing to with it, Elena tells me. On to the changing room, remove our clothes, make-up, jewelry, hairclips even and put them in a locker. In exchange we receive the institutions optional attire — the towel. I can't help feeling my identity, my dignity is being left behind all neatly folded in that small, dark space. The relaxation room is large and everything is painted migraine white. Bodies - pale pink, brown, ashen, fuse in all that brightness, voices blend with sounds of rushing water. We are one, no clues to social status, unsexed, ageless. Nudity is truly democratic. My eyes are opened, yet seem closed. Lunch is strangely sensuous, each taste - kiwi, guava, avocado pear. In the sauna, we become two steaming mounds of flesh that whisper, giggle, then fall silent, sometimes limp and breathless, finally red-faced and oblivious. We are obliged to leave, exiled to the shower, redefined in vague, human form, then propelled still dazed and tingling toward the pool. Dive in. Calm returns, enfolds us and we glide in unison across the length and breadth of our pre-fabricated paradise. Elena goes for a massage. I stay, tread water endlessly, entranced by weightless limbs, their rhythm, the cool waves of pleasure rising from my feet and breaking on my face in tender ripples. The bell rings. Back to the changing room, lockers open, identities unfold - black, white, multi-colored underwear, elaborate dresses, neat suits, jeans and T-shirts, high heels, heavy boots or running shoes. The spectacle. We are visible again, lining up along the row of mirrors for confirmation while the din of hairdryers and heated rollers mounts. And the smell of dignity and perfume fills the air.

Érotisme

A bedroom scene, but not as I intended. Didn't have time to get the curtains or put away the clothes. The room is ugly, it depresses me. "Pretend you're somewhere else," he tries to humor me. I want to laugh, but can't. The light is wrong, so harsh, must turn it off – the chaos, the winter pallor obliterated by the darkness. No, sunlight is best, the skin glows in a certain way. I prefer the afternoon. "But I won't be here then," he whispers in my ear, voice gentle, warm. If only it was summer, windows would be open, blinds flapping in the breeze. It's cold in here. "I'll turn the heat on," he is patient, understanding. I am difficult. I don't know why. Perhaps, I should be wearing something else – a sheer, black, silky something, a little perfume, comb my hair? Mirror, mirror.... The illusion, still important after all these years. I look awful. "No, you don't," his hands around my waist. I want to feel the weight, the strange abrasive surface, the delicious difference and yet, I am not re-conciled. I need to know, a word, a look. Who is the fairest.... Please talk to me. He is on stage. He senses it, "I haven't got the script."

E XTASE

Meeting at the station again, always in a hurry. Sarah and I are having coffee, both wearing jeans and commiserating with one another on their lack of status in the eyes of our fashion conscious offspring. "She made fun of me you know," Sarah grumbles, "when I asked her if it was my clothes, she told me, 'No Mom, its the total look.'" I smile and say, "I know exactly what you mean. All the intricacies of the current dress code were explained to me last week; it seems that mods wear monkey boots but don't like punks who go in for studs and make a point of loathing everyone especially casuals who can't do without authentic labels, and despise the snides who try to fake it. When I asked him where I would fit into this, he told me, 'Nowhere Mom, you're too old to be anything'." Sarah laughs so loudly it rejuvenates me. "Yes, I'm sure we will survive this phase as we have all the others, but why, I wonder, do I buy him almost anything he wants, I mean expensive clothes I would never buy myself and then to make it worse, I have to wash them out by hand. At times I see myself as some low ranking member of an esoteric cult preparing vestments for boy priests who worship leisure gods like Nike." "Don't worry," she consoles me, "didn't Freud say somewhere, clothes have great significance for children and they should be taken seriously?" I am relieved, "Must admit. I do adore him, makes me happy seeing him so young and perfect." Sarah nods, "It's true," she says, "with Gayle as well, I have been shocked, but usually I'm completely fascinated by the way she looks. There was a time, I guess around sixteen, when she took over. Then it seemed ridiculous for me to even try. What's more, it doesn't matter now. I just like looking."

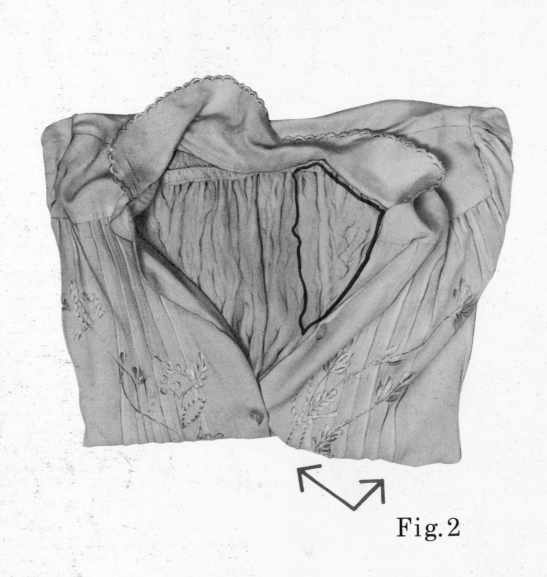

Fig.2

EXTASE

The first week of September and already, leaves are falling. An ominous sign, mother would say. She is not well, has been in pain the last two days. Can't convince her to take the tablets. She's superstitious, declares, "That killed your father." I argue, "It was more than that, please take them, it might help you, it would help me too if you could go to sleep. I'm tired, came home for a rest, wanted someone to look after me. Instead she is the child. Feel cheated, angry, then repentant. Call the doctor, say its urgent. He agrees to an appointment but not till four o'clock. I try to make her comfortable. She says she is afraid, afraid of being alone, afraid of imposing on her friends, afraid of being neglected, of suffering, dying..." "Mother, don't," I ask her to get ready even though it's early. I am afraid, afraid her fear will be contagious. Then, in spite of everything, she insists on getting dressed the way she always has as long as I can remember, "to the teeth". Her auburn hair immobilized with spray, brown eyebrow-pencil, lipstick - coral pink, the crisp white summer dress. And the stilettos. I protest, "you can hardly walk, you can't wear those". She is stubborn, resplendent even in defiance. More than mere appearance, I can see that now, its to do with heroes dressed for battle, willing to go on. And after all, she is still very beautiful. I love her, but I want to leave. At the clinic, he is patronizing and evasive, diagnosis - a pinched nerve perhaps, don't know, don't worry, take this. At home again, she tells me that's the worst part, insecurity, not knowing. "No truth anyway," I lecture, "only theories, treatments, changing all the time." No consolation either. I can see she isn't listening, staring past me toward the lake - serene and still, reflecting every minute detail of the shoreline, inverted like a memory and more enticing than the thing itself. She looks at me, "to be an older woman is..." she pauses, "beyond words, can't describe it. I don't mean not feeling well, you can adjust to that, it's something else I think, like not being taken seriously by doctors or solicitors, not even by my analyst." "Dora's mother," I say, talking to myself. "Who?" she asks. "Never mind," I put my arms around her. The picture on the lake is saturated with magenta - a familiar ending for so many evenings just like this one. Yet the stillness is disconcerting.

Extase

The white dress is part of a plot to escape. From what I'm not quite sure, but all through the cold, dark and indifferent winter I have been planning it. Learned academic by day, and by night, secret reader of holiday brochures and eater of maple sugar candy, planning how the three of us would meet in Miami, happy family reunited - father, mother, child, against a backdrop of blue sky and pounding surf of course. I have told no one. Finally, the day arrives. I pack the suitcase with devotion, the way a bride would do her trousseau: no jeans, no boots, no leather jacket or coat of any kind and nothing black, only brightly colored blouses, loosely fitting trousers, shorts, halters, high-heeled shoes and all the jewelry I ever wanted to wear and didn't have a chance to. And the dress. I refuse to wear a coat even to the airport in anticipation of the happy metamorphosis that will inevitably take place when I emerge eight hours later. And it does. The air is hot and thick. I feel it soldering the bits and pieces of my body into something tangible, entire. I can be seen, imagine men are looking at me, even look at them sometimes. Soon, they arrive, seem much shorter, fatter, whiter than I had remembered, but it doesn't matter. We are together, I am glad. What's more, today is Easter Sunday. Naturally, I'm wearing the white dress — simple, silk, embroidered bodice, gathered at the waist, full skirt falling just below my knee, and thinking, thank god no one will see me, (I mean everyone is in New York), and wonder who am I wearing this for anyway. Not him, he doesn't notice and the prospect of negotiating Disneyland has already given him a headache. Then my angelic son tells everyone, "look at my Mommy". The riddle solved. I am transported in a halo of fluorescent light to the land of "good-enough-mothers." The motel manager waves his magic wand and says, "Please come with me into the dining room where you will feast on champagne, strawberries and cream, the Seven Dwarfs will play the Brandenburg Concertos and I'm quite sure you will live happily ever after." And we do.

Lenders to the exhibition:
The Tate Gallery
The Arts Council of Great Britain
New Hall, University of Cambridge

Photographs by Ray Barrie and F.H. Marlow
Illustrations for *Corpus* courtesy the artist